THE BLACK-OUT BOOK

THE BLACK-OUT BOOK

Peter Carpenter

2002

Published by Arc Publications
Nanholme Mill, Shaw Wood Road
Todmorden, Lancs. OL14 6DA, UK

Copyright © Peter Carpenter 2002

Design by Tony Ward
Printed at the Arc & Throstle Press
Nanholme Mill, Todmorden, Lancs.

ISBN 1 900072 69 6

Acknowledgements are due to the editors of the following publications where some of these poems or versions of them first appeared: *English*, *The Rialto*, *Metre*, the *Independent*, *The Shop*, *The Tabla Book of New Verse* (1999, 2000 & 2002), *Smiths Knoll*, *Navis*, *Other Poetry*, *Orbis*, *Fire*; the poem 'Tag' was commissioned as part of the Maidstone Millennium River Park development; 'Ejects Stars' appeared in *Poetry South East 2000* (Frogmore Press); 'East Coast Haiku' in *River* (Medway Arts); 'Middle Distance' and 'Peaceline' appeared in the chap-book *No Age* (Shoestring 2001); 'Potato Junkers' in *Choosing an England* (Worple 1997).

The publishers acknowledge financial assistance from Yorkshire Arts Board

CONTENTS

SCHRÄGMUSIK

Fix / 9

Potato Junkers / 14
Son / 16
Contrails / 17
Cuckoo / 18
Middle Distance / 20
Royal Doulton / 21
All Clear / 23
The Bloomsbury Front / 24
Poetry of the thirties / 24
Sea Defences / 25
The Dimension of the Present Moment / 26

EJECTS STARS

The Sun / 29
No fit state / 30
Peaceline / 31
Concealed Entrance / 32
Yesterday's Solution / 33
Cuttings / 34
Old Ground / 35
Claire's Knee / 36
Westerly / 37
East Coast Haiku / 38
No Prizes / 39
Ejects Stars / 40

Tag / 41

*

Notes / 42

For my mother and father

Schrägmusik

FIX

'Crewing up'
                out of darkness
fifty years and more
of radio silence
            I trace a course
visibility poor

―――

White Christmas
          on a gramophone
somewhere distant
pinpoints
           fixes
  dot to dot
(navigation lights off)

we're for Köln

―――

I take my bearings
           climbing
echo to echo
      Charleroi Namur
Grasmere   Ilfracombe
    the Wash
  (self as centre)

―――

   climbing
        Kingston by-pass
A3 flyover   Decca building
  Escort passenger side
cuts us up
           steady now
force him over   terrorise

   now where was I

  Cala Ratjada
sipping at the poolside
    our German neighbour
mentions Gladbach
         'bombed there'

a minor blow
     to diplomatic relations

    18.31   flak?
  Δ bombs gone
beware *Schrägmusik*
185 Gladbach 8   248 Gladbach 11
     255 Gladbach 15

Nippes Marshalling Yards
    'tonight without fail'
just like   *the ones*
   sleigh bells
         ringing

           checklist: Mae West   sub mariner's sweater
                              silks   harness
chart
      pinned to table

      (self as centre)

                        ———

second can get you out of trouble
           out and then
in when you're cornering   see there you are
           trying to save my life again
pilot head iced up   airspeed unknown
              Leeds Loughton
         M1   M11

                        ———

North Foreland 29
     Selsey Bill   marble clack
         pebble gradations

    bottom bottom bugger
                    bugger
              bottom
    sod

          the cracked leather
the *Imp* or the *Popular*
       behave you two
right
     okay   we're stopping the car

                        ———

clean through lights on red
        in Laval
    wrong side of the road
cruising in top
    one hundred and fifty five
nautical miles per hour
    by my calculations

———

I repeat   I am a ni-hil-ist
        to anybody out there
in *The Crosby*
        The Oswald The Bluebell
   (rough that last one)
I've been meaning to do this for years

   O my blood brothers

———

   weed-cracked runway
ghost squadron   'ah   Elsham 'crewing up'
   out of darkness
Forbes Westcott Armstrong
   visibility poor

O my blood brothers

   the many men   you know you know

———

accelerate out of trouble
        (we're for Köln)
airspeed unknown
somewhere distant
        on a gramophone

———

    always have somewhere to go
          Ewell Tech   Ebbisham   St. Martin's
              Nonsuch   Cheam
hi-ho silver lining
        commence homing
      never reaching the end

  dawn is mauve
            not grey

———

or *Stille Nacht*
   faces lit
      from below
masses   dressing trees
        mouthing at candles
            incendiaries

———

fire the size of Hyde Park
        some terrible revenge thing

———

        hey you there
              with the glasses
already celebrating
   *you're gonna reap just what
you sow*
        not one of them knows
     where I'm coming from

POTATO JUNKERS
Elsham Wolds, Lincolnshire 1994

Chin so near I could smell the last meal
on his breath. Just past his left ear a Lancaster
is rising above the human gougings towards Scunny
over the wolds. It subdues distance.

'You're a stubborn bastard, Flight Sergeant.'
I nod. (Never was one for self-promotion.)
'Now, peel them.'
                      I survey the world
of potatoes in the vat of water before me:
every spud a handful in the semi-cloud
of its own making; the point of my scraper
creases the tension. Primary target:
any old King Edward's from the surfaces
clustering. I prong one. Feel the dribble
of attachments in my palm. I bomb it back
and pause until the slightly frothy rocking
calms. Check visibility, air speed. Then
I hit on it.
              Again I pick out my spud
and give it a stare. And keep going until
it's a hundred yards wide. It becomes a city.
I pinpoint its tuberous spires, start
to flatten vulnerable settlements
and define its centre with my blade. Hours
of it. I grow to admire it. It gives only
after silent resistance. There'll be no
tearful ringing crises: it's no onion.
Even as I bust it down from snowball to
goitre to marble there's no reaction.
It glistens. In perfect shape. That's it.
I pop it back into the vat and wait.

That night I dip into another world:
I navigate above a scalding tureen.
We've been to Stettin. Gardening. Don't let on
but Orford and Gladbach keep changing
latitude and there's a knife in my hand.
We're trapped in a beam
                        a hundred yards wide.
Foundries burn below.

                    I wake to echoes
from around the station as hailstones
the size of potatoes hit the roof.

(Note: 'gardening' was slang for a mining raid in WW2)

SON

Hanging up there – dad's old coat.
                                          A real one
this, Aberdeen Crombie 'post-war heavy duty
allegiance' weave. The stuff of long-standing
family rows.
                  Fat trapped from Christmases
deep in its tough system of greenish flecks –
an age after the slush of sprouts and roast
has been cleared away. And you're in there.

I breathe hard. Getting heavy now.
                                From solo
late night tramps, in you clump. We share the draught –
your bearing tells me it straight:
                            son,
that's what I bloody mean by inspiration.

Our front-door vibrates. Five pints to the good
    I sniff into
               a sweat-darkened lining.
Now, I just about carry it off.

CONTRAILS

Chalk paths
through waist-high grasses

seeding ways
above the skylark

the roaring
a lonely impulse

over fairways and rough
visible breath

London from the downs
an empty gas-holder

Tolworth Tower
all adolescence

these quick rivers
their own spring-line

CUCKOO

Monday

and Nanna Cuckoo
presided over the line, drying
weather or not, occupying
the kitchen: a vast tent
of sounds, belongings.

'Cuckoo'

her calling card
with knuckled rap at the veiled pane
of the backdoor.
Hawk nose, hour-glass calves
bandaged

(Cuckoo)

turban-style,
raincoat on indoors
'just in case'; playing to win
at chess, cracking down flush or run
at whist, lifting pieces

(Cuckoo)

at dominoes, making me howl
'not fair, not fair.' She was cold meat, mashed
potatoes, huge scrapings
of chair legs, tea thick with sugar.
Then her death:

(Cuckoo)

the niff from tins
of humbrol paints, glue,
thinners for my Airfix kits;
and the way she looked one Boxing Day
from our car back to

our house, told father
that she knew a family who lived there too,
called him Bill not Pete.
We didn't see his tears. He practised
his golfswing

in the back garden
whistling replica *air flo* balls away up
into the hedge off
a doormat shredding from the impact
of each shot

until the light started to go;
foraged in privet and hawthorn
for 'stock', some crushed, some
lost for good, hacking
around with a three iron

into leaf-showers
sawdust-dry, trying
not to hear
a voice fluttering, telling him over
and over it was only her going

Cuckoo

        Cuckoo

Cuckoo

MIDDLE DISTANCE

Mother around
        the war years:
grainy snapshots.

    There tap-dancing
on the kitchen table

or evacuee in Wales
    scrubbing a doorstep
with her sister Vi
               or this one
running the one hundred
            and ten yards final
barefoot at the old White City

and here
    I cannot tell the fake
stocking seams
(eyeliner ankle to hem) from the real thing.

Interior.
        Thomas Marsh's Cheese Shop,
Bishopsgate. It could be her
marking time in the queue

for crumbly mature slithers
to drop into a hand
of grease-proofed paper

away from the wire. It's eating
into the hard rind,
                the press

of coats, veined marble,
the split-second smiles
as another turns on her heel.

ROYAL DOULTON

She's back. House in the dark.
I hear an engine cut, steps,
the front door. Pause, then
prink-prink in the kitchen:
harsh strip to delineate
sink unit, lino, all of it.

I sit on the stairs just past
my bedtime. Cup of tea:
milk from the fridge, top drawer
that sticks, clink
of apostle spoons, larder
for hanging cup, then saucer.

Enter: mother, cup
from our service,
Royal Doulton, in hand. A crack,
I notice, delicate
as a hair, right up
to the rim, beneath the glaze

a brownish-grey. A pattern
in blue on white. Daughter
and grandson stare. Then a shriek,
mighty, constant. She flicks
the kettle's whistle
from the throat. Remembers

one for the pot. Water onto
dark, dry leaves, there
in tannin-stained china.
Strong stuff. A steady pour.
She's finding ways to put it,
a crack rising to her lips.

ALL CLEAR

This is London
    breaking into light

appliances working the Thames

    a double decker
advertising Schweppes

THE BLOOMSBURY FRONT

The old loves, arm in arm, shuffle
dust up a track past the fruit farm
years away from that governess
who made them eat greens, say grace.
Nothing here, they swore, would come
to harm. Stickers for *White Star Line*
and *Cunard* patch a grip. One of the men
does the honours for a sundowner
and the finest minds go under with 'just
a dash' of soda. Art is not life. Sitters eye
the tantulus while bruised early fallers
lie cidrous up to the first frost. Another
rooster is stencilled on a crib. Each siesta
Rebecca fingers a flesh-trenched bud
in dreams of the other ranks standing easy
after a great-coated king's inspection.

Death's a distant operator who asks
each caller to 'hold' for Ripe 269.

POETRY OF THE THIRTIES

Those blue-prints that would map out a Europe?
They've gone: letter-bundles
in rubber bands: near on a decade
of domesticity tied up
in phone exchanges, occasional
prose, snaps from the front. Can there be another
such weekend (mood-swings, the rain, relations)?

They grow on us. Lines of heart and life
revisit declarations. Suddenly we're here,
sheltering behind a dry stone wall
in the Lakes after a long walk with time
to ponder cloud formations,
expecting soon a drizzle
to shade the planner's dream.

SEA DEFENCES

red admirals
     ground elder
  is it

    sandpipers
oystercatchers

listen   really
    listen

cattle
     a bale of straw
shingle
     Weybourne
  the settlement

  flint-napped
defences   abandoned
     anti-landing gear

from the last war
          a way forward
a sounding

THE DIMENSION OF THE PRESENT MOMENT
i.m. Miroslav Holub

An aggregation of cells
examined under
the microscope
on this slide:

the stir
of things working
into their
own pattern.

Like Stubbs
at the knacker's yard,
or Ruskin
by the waterfall

each is its own
domain, subject
and object, complete
in movement.

These, your miniatures,
might yet regain
the taken city,
salvage the plunder,

tend to the horse's spillage.
Every last drop
is held in
their surface tension

and for us
they live.

Ejects Stars

THE SUN

Out where Austrian blinds open
onto a ribbon development
past new-insured rooftops
along the Godstone valley
you deliver yourself each dawn.

Father of total block,
delineator of rose and turd,
patroniser of asylum seekers,
slow there for the sleeping policeman,
caricature the foraging beggar!

Semtex-planter and blanket-bomber
of Docklands and Spaghetti Junction,
dogged graffiti artist, tagger of highrise
and semi, pledged laureate, pronounce
now upon the restoration of Windsor!

NO FIT STATE

We're going places. We've been told.
Numbed by the across and down?
Swap places with the next man.
Number his days. Button up.
We're going places. We've been told.
Families, individuals, that's all.

Fantasies toadstool. We all need
some degradation. Swap places.
Personal details. Button up.
We're going places. We've been told.
King's Cross. An occupied booth.
Families, individuals, that's all.

Clouds hold. A depression appeared
to threaten. Fantasies toadstool.
We're going places. We've been told.
Businessmen are pucker. Button up.
Play area, compound. A likely story.
Families, individuals, that's all.

Shop fronts remind. Asphalt dries.
We're going places. We've been told.
We all need some degradation.
King's Cross. A likely story.
Trees trade in orange for green.
Families, individuals, that's all.

The first body bag. Degradation.
Fantasies, pucker shop fronts,
asphalt. We all need some. Swap
places. Personal details. Button up.
We're going places, we've been told.
Families, individuals. That's all.

1982

PEACELINE

Two boys stare each other out,
locked into trainers, t-shirts,
those labels that distinguish
a *Lacoste* from a *Nike*,

crocodiles from a tick;
forcing milk teeth grins,
absorbing snot, saliva,
the tiny differences;

and the prospect of failure
forces a glare to resist
that unthinkable concession
to darkness, the first blink.

CONCEALED ENTRANCE

Steady progress north from the city.
Larchfield, Kirkmoyle are names you clarify,
these, your old childhood haunts,
where they still dig for bog oak.

Highlights from Verdi and Puccini
fill the front seats with Maria Callas;
we run past the castle at Dunluce
on from Portrush in a constant mizzle

and there's a pause, after whitewashed
outhouses, holiday homes in Bushmills,
concealed entrances to lounge bars,
a marking of time in the wipers

or our talk or the end of the human
settlements along the coast, that we use
to study the breakers, the drag,
vegetation mottled and uprooted

even as we eye the waves,
contemplate what it is to live
on such an island with, all the time,
this power, waiting at our leisure,

marking out its territory in foam,
tearing back into itself before
occupying the sand, again drawn
into it, again giving us pause.

YESTERDAY'S SOLUTION

Away from the discipline of the true coast road
where each verge reveals the sea's sheer hold
we emerge onto the M2 past Ballymoney, Ballymena,
immersed in those clues that just won't come easy.
Through the haze we'd imagined waves off Rathlin.
We braved the tide-line and a frothed cold swim,
putty-white toes leaving their marks in wet sand.
Now along the Lagan up to Queen's Bridge the sides
of houses and miles of scrap are innocently defined
by growing shadow. We sit in traffic. Some drivers
stretch their legs, switch off. An evening breeze twitches
loud ties. In that tough last corner 'adamant' might just fit.
A controlled explosion tremors across the water.
Ambulances mount the kerb. We mouth 'Jesus Christ'
and register the smoke's sudden, obvious meaning.
Diversions follow peace-lines, draw us all into the night.

The next morning we head back into the centre
past men who rake layers of tarmac. A cauldron
of pitch is stirred. It steams. We look for the solution
in today's paper. There. The words we didn't get.

CUTTINGS

All part of the search for killers, the car,
the one used for the trip from Carrickmacross,
the Omagh one, the one detonated two days after.
For good reasons then this police poster
from a photograph taken just seconds prior
to the detonation, with all the human figures

blanked out, as though scissors had worked
round their legs and arms and heads, to focus
vision on the numberplate of the car
in question, the one from Carrickmacross,
the Omagh one, detonated just seconds after.
All part of a search past the blanks, the car,

over grey tiles, building shadow, shopfronts
(*Beauty Salon, The Kozy Corner, Florist*)
on to trees and tiny safe flecks too distant
to identify, before the eye can return
to white clumps round the car, the Omagh one,
there, the stilled voids, the held outline

of child on adult shoulders, as though
scissors had worked round legs, arms, heads,
for some good reason, prior to the detonation.

OLD GROUND

You again. Little wonder.
Back to do your strange little number:
twelve years late, mid-November.
Down to Walton Pond.
There, what you knew you'd find:
the fond couples, children throwing crusts
at the water with all the trust
God gave them. Sit on the bench.

Not a tear, surely. Spare us. A branch
shivers. An interior light
flicks on. Homely. How did you delight
in a prospect of this? Whatever next?
Past the house in a couple of circuits
to check the cars on the drive. Regrets?
What right have you to expect
anything but a feel for what's gone,
what's been stuck in your heart too long.

Face it. Now, run along.

CLAIRE'S KNEE
After Lowell

This might be the future – sewage plant,
trout farm, cress beds, a necking pair
of swans on the Chess, Frazer's old banger
cornering at fifty past *The Elephant*,
while we two lie, head to head,
perusing all our Sundays – till death.
I repeat by heart... *How can you say
I go about things the wrong way...*

This might be a heaven. One May
we trembled at the caress
of a breeze that deadheaded dandelions
over bus shelters and double yellows
down the Holloway Road.
The 'Burbs one airless matinee
then at night the performance of the lovers
of our damp lives, those slugs defining
their last moments in *Saxa* trails on lino...

My head's not straight. Every night
(Dobbin, Tole, *1664*) is a 'big night'
still hanging over us, your 'Merrie England'
resurrected, my old love, as the credits
for a Rohmer movie run, and you disengage
my fingers from your knee.

The Northern Line keeps us both, we two,
pretending to read, marking a place,
on opposite platforms, in shudders
of dead air, until a connection comes
and one of us disappears.

WESTERLY

The sting of vinegar
on wind-chapped lips

white plastic chairs
by the *Galleon* cafe

scots pine bent into
the shape of each gale

a madman in shorts
directing the clouds

with a two-ounce tin
of *St. Bruno's Flake*

mouthing instructions
at stacked drystone walls

windsurfers breaking
across Daymer Bay

sense in spray
the pull of each wave

EAST COAST HAIKU

Laureen's, Falmouth, Cape Cod

Tuna melt. On rye?
Iced water. Enjoy! Finger-
nails chewed to the quick.

Ellis Island

Suitcase full of air.
Vast concentration: faces
against the sky line.

Hartford, Connecticut

so we had some shots
okay it was crazy this
*   guy parading   huge*

NO PRIZES

They keep coming back to me
with the fried onions,
the steady chuntering of the generator,
spillages of oil on albino grass,

the look in the eyes of the candy-floss girls,
the stacks and hot pants girls,
who desired you for a second

to take them behind the fortune-tellers,
the trailers, the dads, the dodgem-poles
sparking, the stilted summer shadows,

out over the defined fairway of the seventh hole,
veiled by trees, up to the lovingly-mown green
and to hold them there, to kiss away all trace
of giving granular sweetness, to sense
a pad of warmth, but not to spoil it, to go too far,

allowing time for the Ferris Wheel to swing out
a scream of London, for Hoop-la, the Ghost Train,
the airgun, the procession of flip-up rabbits
to roll past
           and for the prizes

the doomed goldfish   the giant teddy
an octangular plate in some larder to this day

a hand's moisture   breath clinging to me
the darkness   alive   unclaimed

EJECTS STARS

Gunpowder: the stuff to make it go
Interred between a split lip of soot

and a loop of chicken-wire, in grass
over a foot high on this, our allotment,

by a barrow, upturned, rust-holed.
It had come from the north, like blown

molten glass at, I reckoned,
one hundred thousand miles per hour

or thereabouts. Like a silencer
from a gun I loosed it from its stick.

We received it: a new power.
Our experts traced its course.

A white dream from the year dot
to this. It came away in our hands.

An earwig clambered out, jagged
with Danegeld, forcep-horned.

I recalled my father tracing the line
of Orion's Belt, pronouncing

upon true north. I studied again:
Made in Huddersfield. Touchpaper

a lost ironic twist; an earthed detach;
a cluggy misfire. Instructions gave us

a rocket. *Do Not Hold* and *Ejects Stars*.
We all stood well back, waited.

TAG

This is it, now, a shape cut in time.
It's a tracer line from the year dot

moving on from its first form: a pulse,
a curl in fluid, continuous creation

lightning sketched, a steady course
that cannot be charted or rolled

in fire then beaten out of us.
We follow its orders with a smile,

a double-take, something in the eyes.
It ripples like the bars of a mackerel sky,

dissolves sun into ice, shore into tide.
We cannot break the code, however hard we try.

NOTES

The Black-Out Book takes its title from a book of the same name published in 1939 by Harrap; it was an anthology of jokes, puzzles, poems, etc, compiled by Evelyn August with 'one purpose in mind – to provide the average family with sufficient amusement and entertainment for one hundred and one black-out nights.' It became in turn part of my own bed-time reading. My title has connotations beyond its immediate source.

Schrägmusik was a term given to the angled fire from cannon fixed at eighty degrees on the fuselage of German night-fighters as they stalked Allied bombers from below. The term's wider sense (angled or oblique music, jazz) is equally applicable.

Fix: the title, preoccupations and shape of the poem come from the world of navigation. It is intended as a kind of fantasia charted via place-names, scraps of song, navigational argot and other domestic and historical bearings. Its specific centre is an RAF bombing raid on the Nippes marshalling yards in Köln on Christmas Eve, 1944. It is dedicated to all the men who flew Lancasters in No. 103 Squadron stationed at Elsham Wolds and, in particular, to my father.

Ejects stars: this is the last part of a warning issued by Standard Fireworks that appears on their display rockets.

Cuttings: the poem is about the Omagh bombing of August 15th, 1998, in particular, the police poster displaying the bomber's car where the figures of nearby pedestrians had been cut round and blanked out.

Tag: the poem can be found engraved on the half-dozen twin steel arches of a sculpture by David Annand in the shape of the double helix structure of DNA; the sculpture, 60m by 7m, is in Whatman's Park, Maidstone. One of the many senses of the title applies to a graffiti artist's signature or 'trademark'.

PETER CARPENTER was born in 1957 in Ewell. He read English at Pembroke College, Cambridge, and from 1992 has taught at Tonbridge School, Kent. He is a Visiting Fellow at the University of Warwick, co-editor of Worple Press, and Literary Editor to the estate of William Hayward. His other books of poetry are *Choosing an England* and *No Age*; he is also the co-author with Toby Newton of *At The End of The Day* (A Dictionary of Received Footballing Wisdom). He lives in Kent with his wife and their two young daughters.